Funky Floral Colouring Book Planner

Kay D Johnson

Johnson, Kay D
Funky Floral Colouring Book Planner
ISBN 978-1-989382-03-5 (pbk)

From _____ to _____

Month _____ Year _____

Monday

Tuesday

Wednesday

Thursday

Friday

Saturday

Sunday

From _____ to _____

Month _____ Year _____

Monday

Tuesday

Wednesday

Thursday

Friday

Saturday

Sunday

From _____ to _____

Month _____ Year _____

Monday

Tuesday

Wednesday

Thursday

Friday

Saturday

Sunday

From _____ to _____

Month _____ Year _____

Monday

Tuesday

Wednesday

Thursday

Friday

Saturday

Sunday

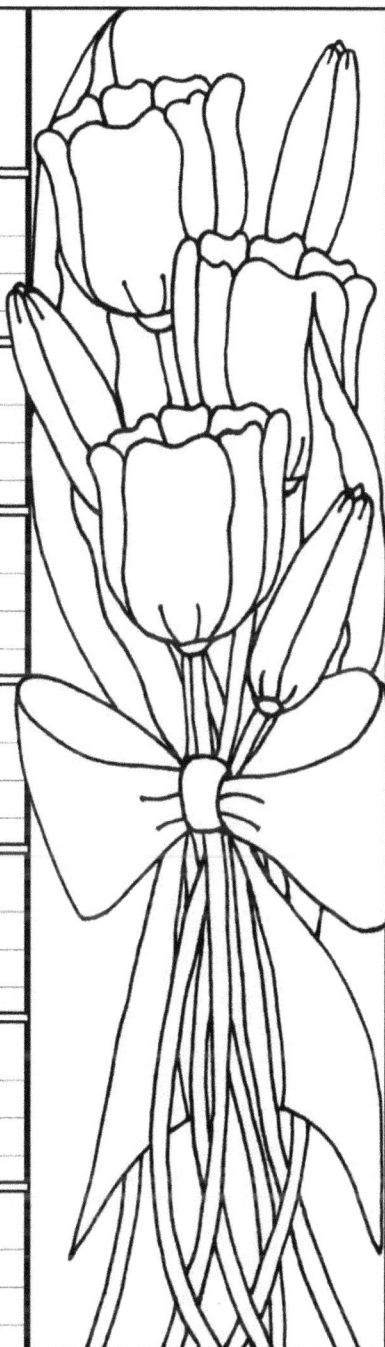

From _____ to _____

Month _____ Year _____

Monday

Tuesday

Wednesday

Thursday

Friday

Saturday

Sunday

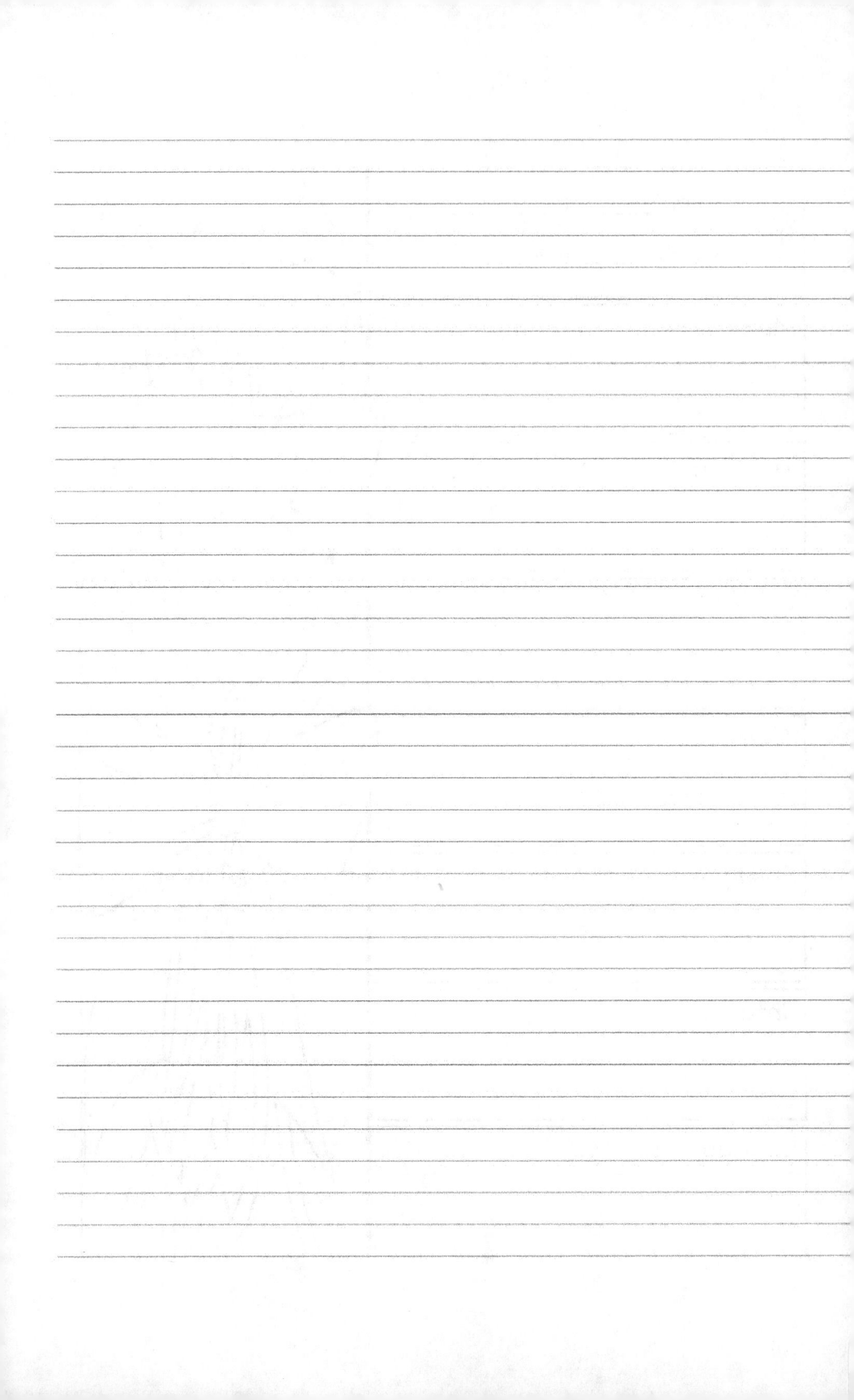

From _____ to _____

Month _____ Year _____

Monday

Tuesday

Wednesday

Thursday

Friday

Saturday

Sunday

From _____ to _____

Month _____ Year _____

Monday

Tuesday

Wednesday

Thursday

Friday

Saturday

Sunday

From _____ to _____

Month _____ Year _____

Monday

Tuesday

Wednesday

Thursday

Friday

Saturday

Sunday

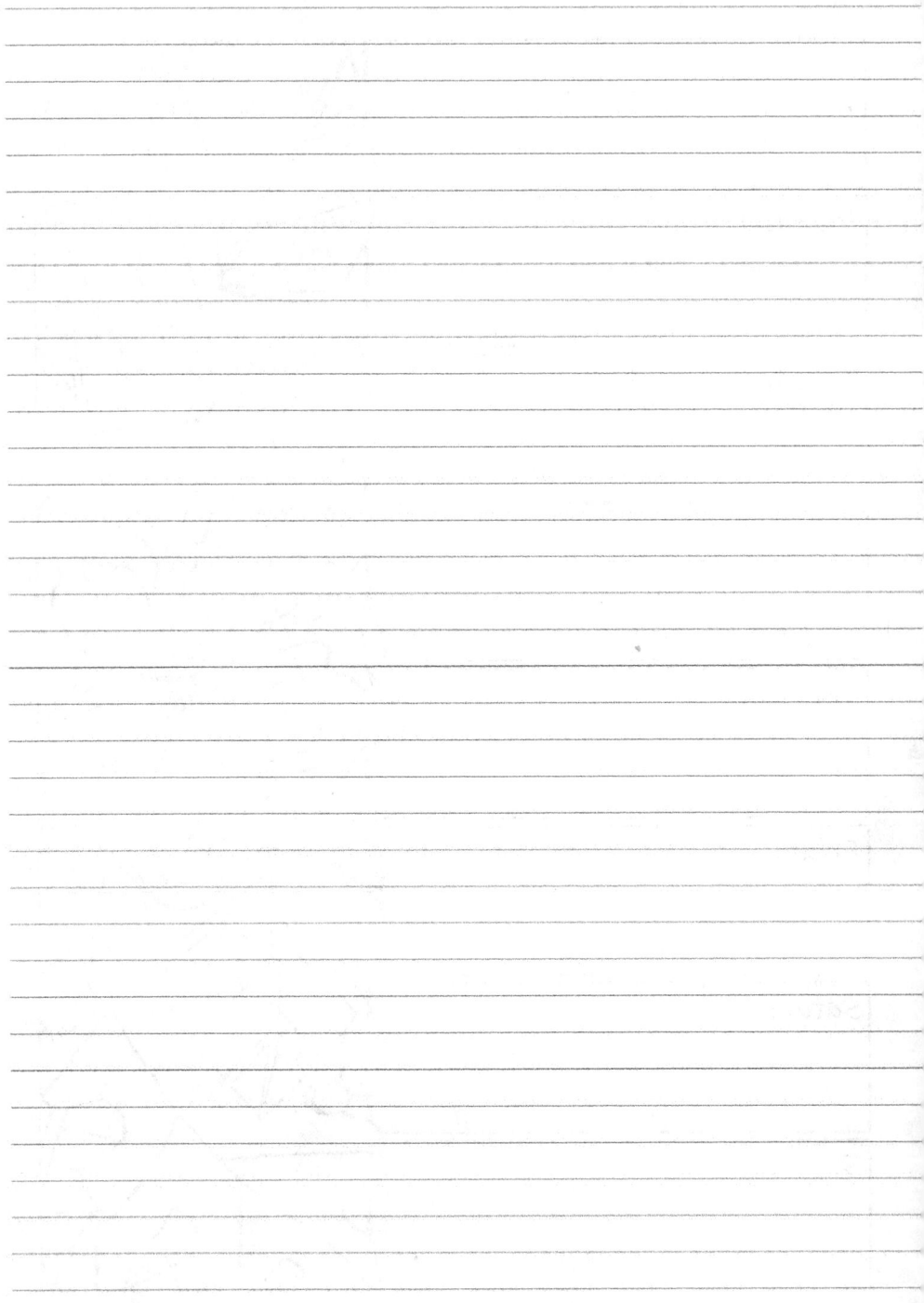

From _____ to _____

Month _____ Year _____

Monday

Tuesday

Wednesday

Thursday

Friday

Saturday

Sunday

From _____ to _____

Month _____ Year _____

Monday

Tuesday

Wednesday

Thursday

Friday

Saturday

Sunday

From _____ to _____

Month _____ Year _____

Monday

Tuesday

Wednesday

Thursday

Friday

Saturday

Sunday

From _____ to _____

Month _____ Year _____

Monday

Tuesday

Wednesday

Thursday

Friday

Saturday

Sunday

From _____ to _____

Month _____ Year _____

Monday

Tuesday

Wednesday

Thursday

Friday

Saturday

Sunday

From _____ to _____

Month _____ Year _____

Monday

Tuesday

Wednesday

Thursday

Friday

Saturday

Sunday

From _____ to _____

Month _____ Year _____

Monday

Tuesday

Wednesday

Thursday

Friday

Saturday

Sunday

From _____ to _____

Month _____ Year _____

Monday

Tuesday

Wednesday

Thursday

Friday

Saturday

Sunday

From _____ to _____

Month _____ Year _____

Monday

Tuesday

Wednesday

Thursday

Friday

Saturday

Sunday

From _____ to _____

Month _____ Year _____

Monday

Tuesday

Wednesday

Thursday

Friday

Saturday

Sunday

From _____ to _____

Month _____ Year _____

Monday

Tuesday

Wednesday

Thursday

Friday

Saturday

Sunday

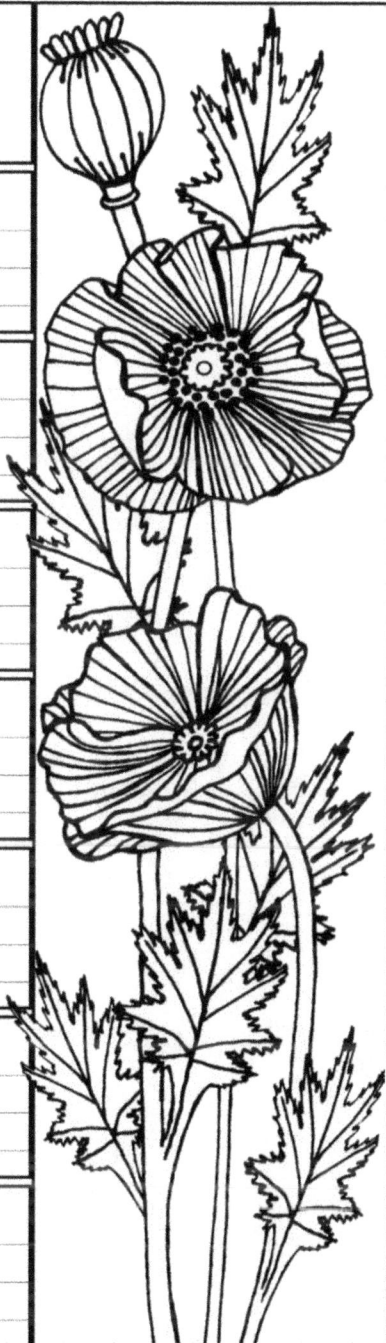

From _____ to _____

Month _____ Year _____

Monday

Tuesday

Wednesday

Thursday

Friday

Saturday

Sunday

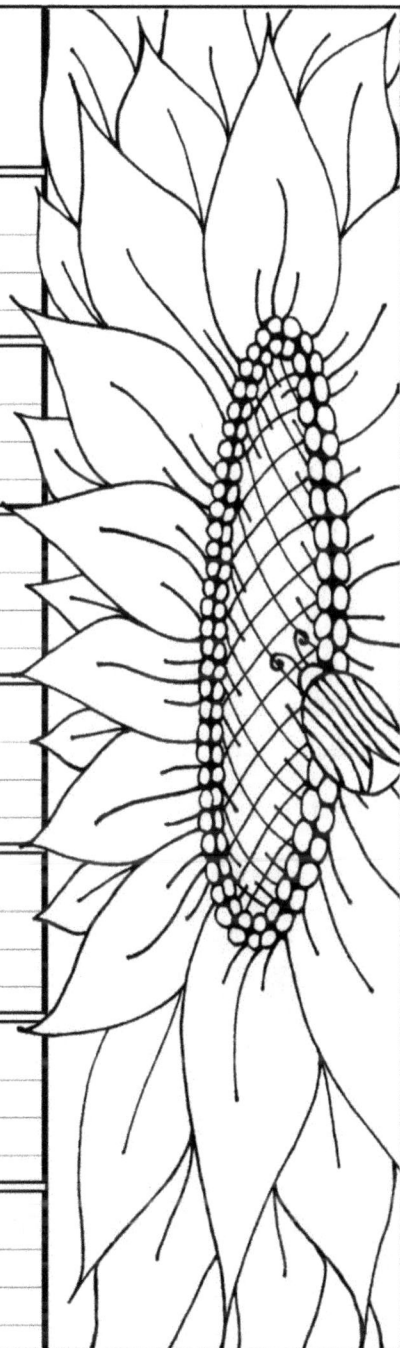

From _____ to _____

Month _____ Year _____

Monday

Tuesday

Wednesday

Thursday

Friday

Saturday

Sunday

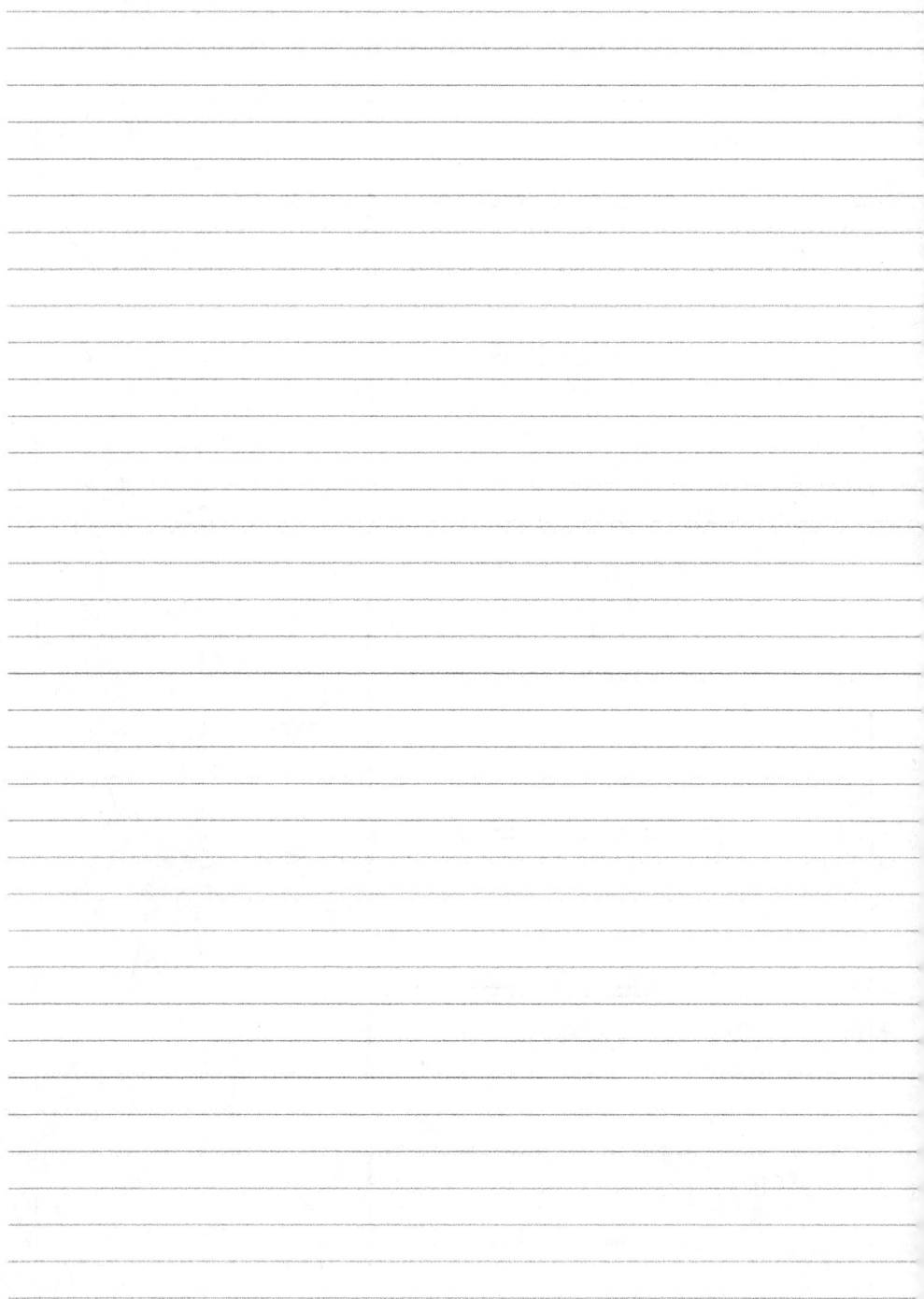

From _____ to _____

Month _____ Year _____

Monday

Tuesday

Wednesday

Thursday

Friday

Saturday

Sunday

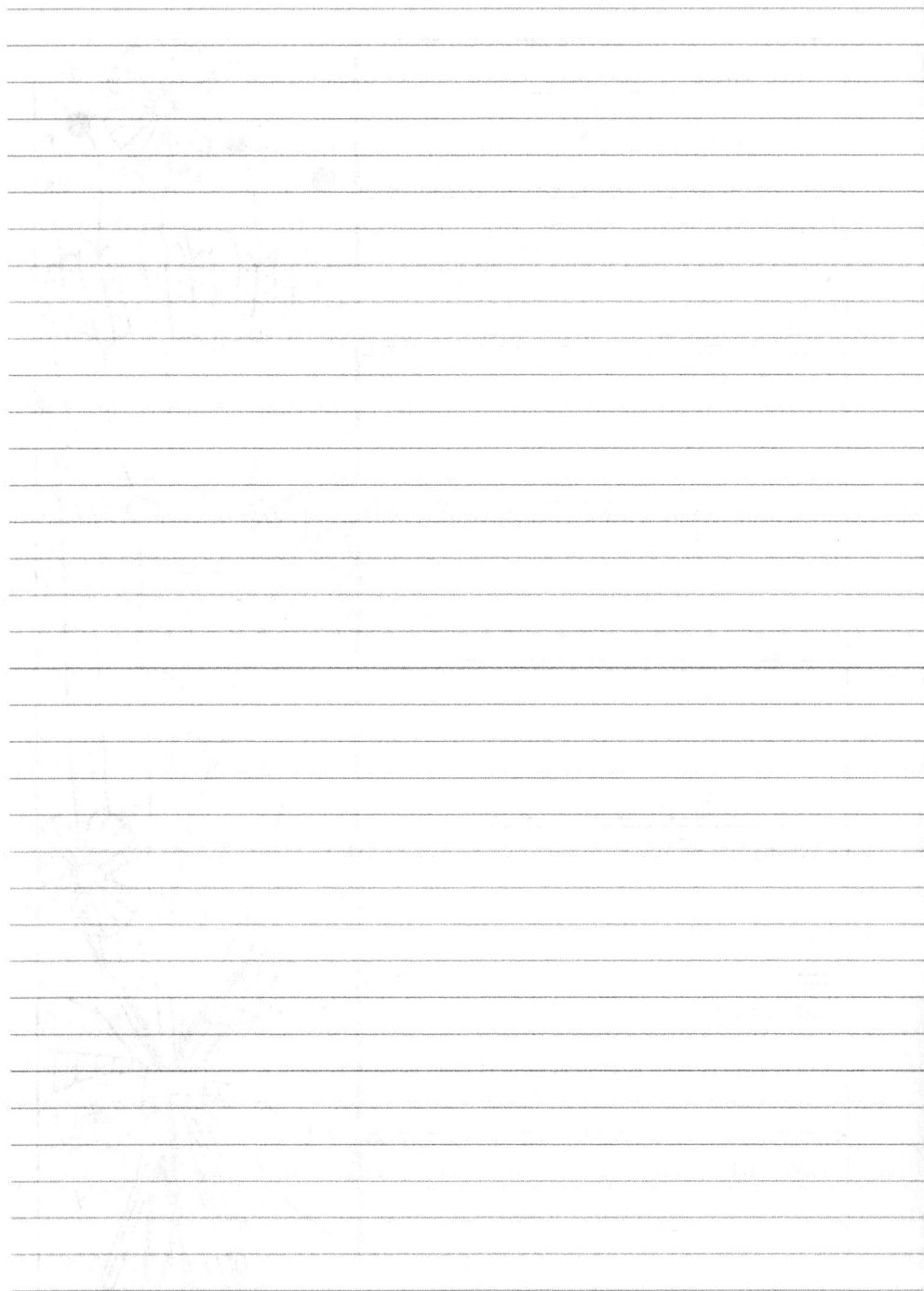

From _____ to _____

Month _____ Year _____

Monday

Tuesday

Wednesday

Thursday

Friday

Saturday

Sunday

From _____ to _____

Month _____ Year _____

Monday

Tuesday

Wednesday

Thursday

Friday

Saturday

Sunday

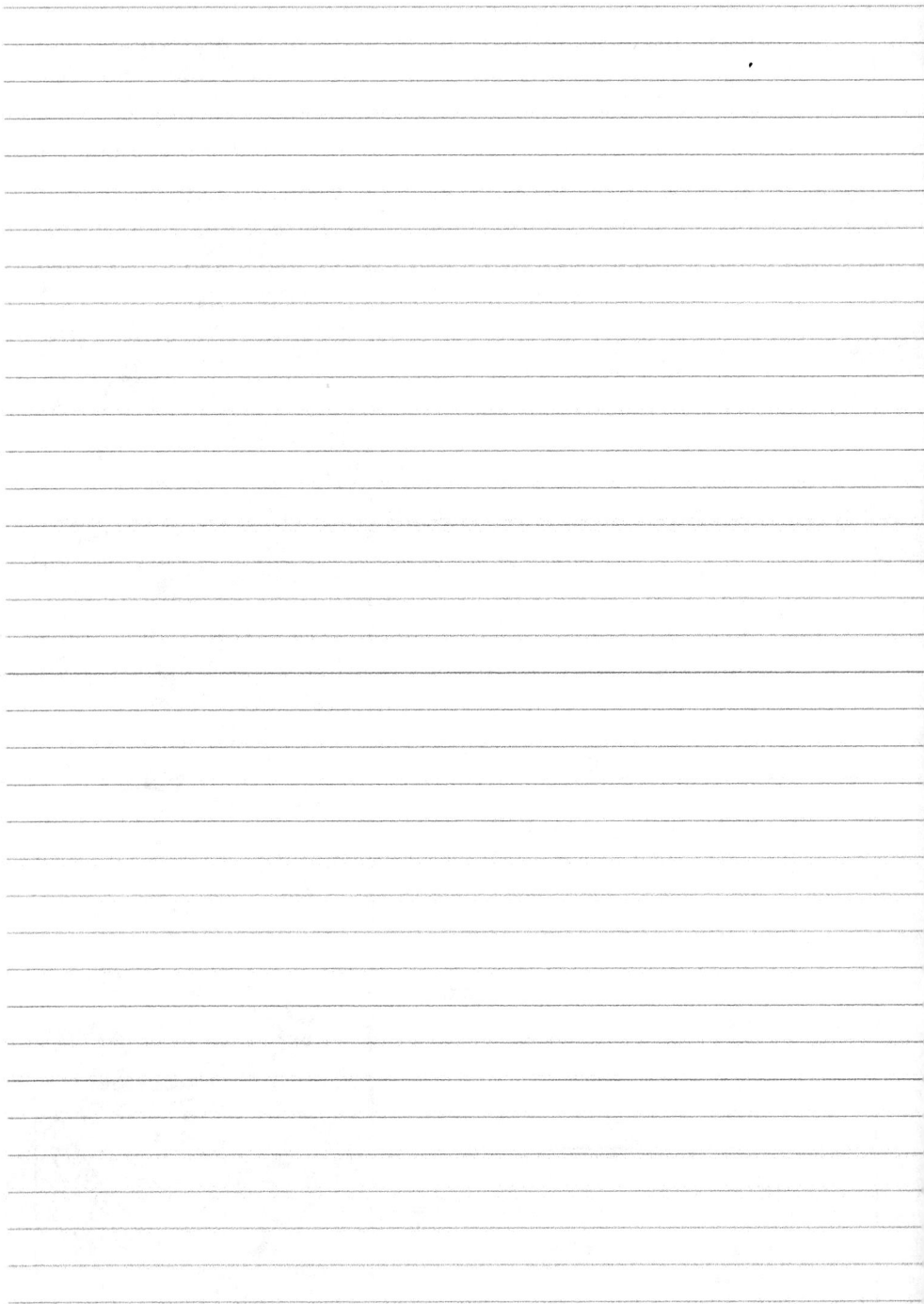

From _____ to _____

Month _____ Year _____

Monday

Tuesday

Wednesday

Thursday

Friday

Saturday

Sunday

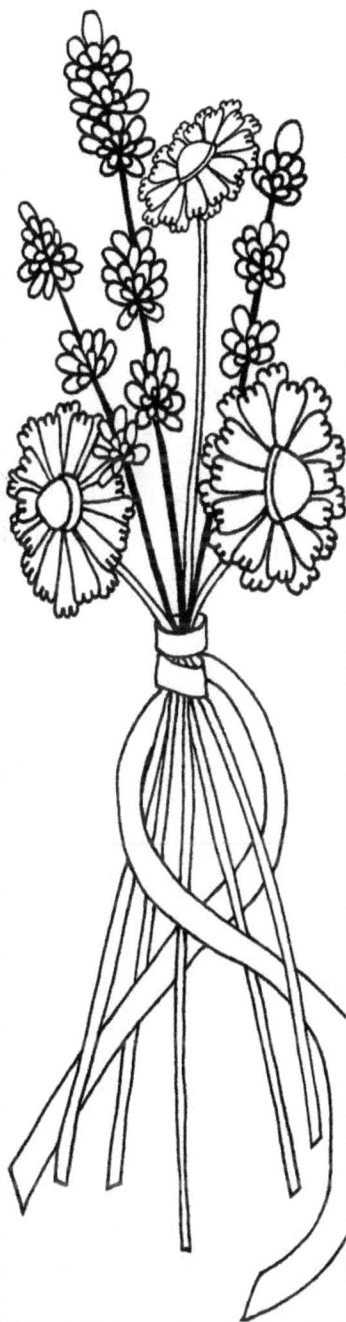

From _____ to _____

Month _____ Year _____

Monday

Tuesday

Wednesday

Thursday

Friday

Saturday

Sunday

From _____ to _____

Month _____ Year _____

Monday

Tuesday

Wednesday

Thursday

Friday

Saturday

Sunday

From _____ to _____

Month _____ Year _____

Monday

Tuesday

Wednesday

Thursday

Friday

Saturday

Sunday

From _____ to _____

Month _____ Year _____

Monday

Tuesday

Wednesday

Thursday

Friday

Saturday

Sunday

From _____ to _____

Month _____ Year _____

Monday

Tuesday

Wednesday

Thursday

Friday

Saturday

Sunday

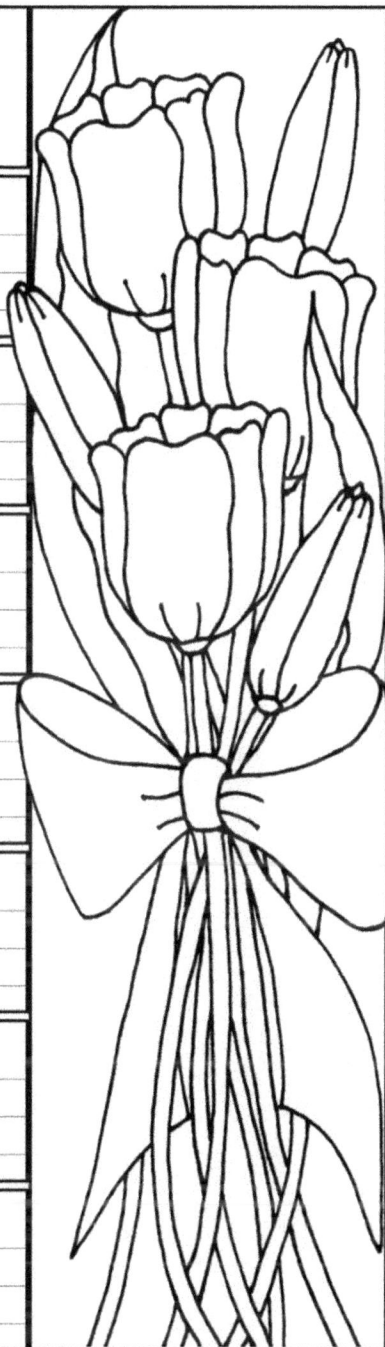

From _____ to _____

Month _____ Year _____

Monday

Tuesday

Wednesday

Thursday

Friday

Saturday

Sunday

From _____ to _____

Month _____ Year _____

Monday

Tuesday

Wednesday

Thursday

Friday

Saturday

Sunday

From _____ to _____

Month _____ Year _____

Monday

Tuesday

Wednesday

Thursday

Friday

Saturday

Sunday

From _____ to _____

Month _____ Year _____

Monday

Tuesday

Wednesday

Thursday

Friday

Saturday

Sunday

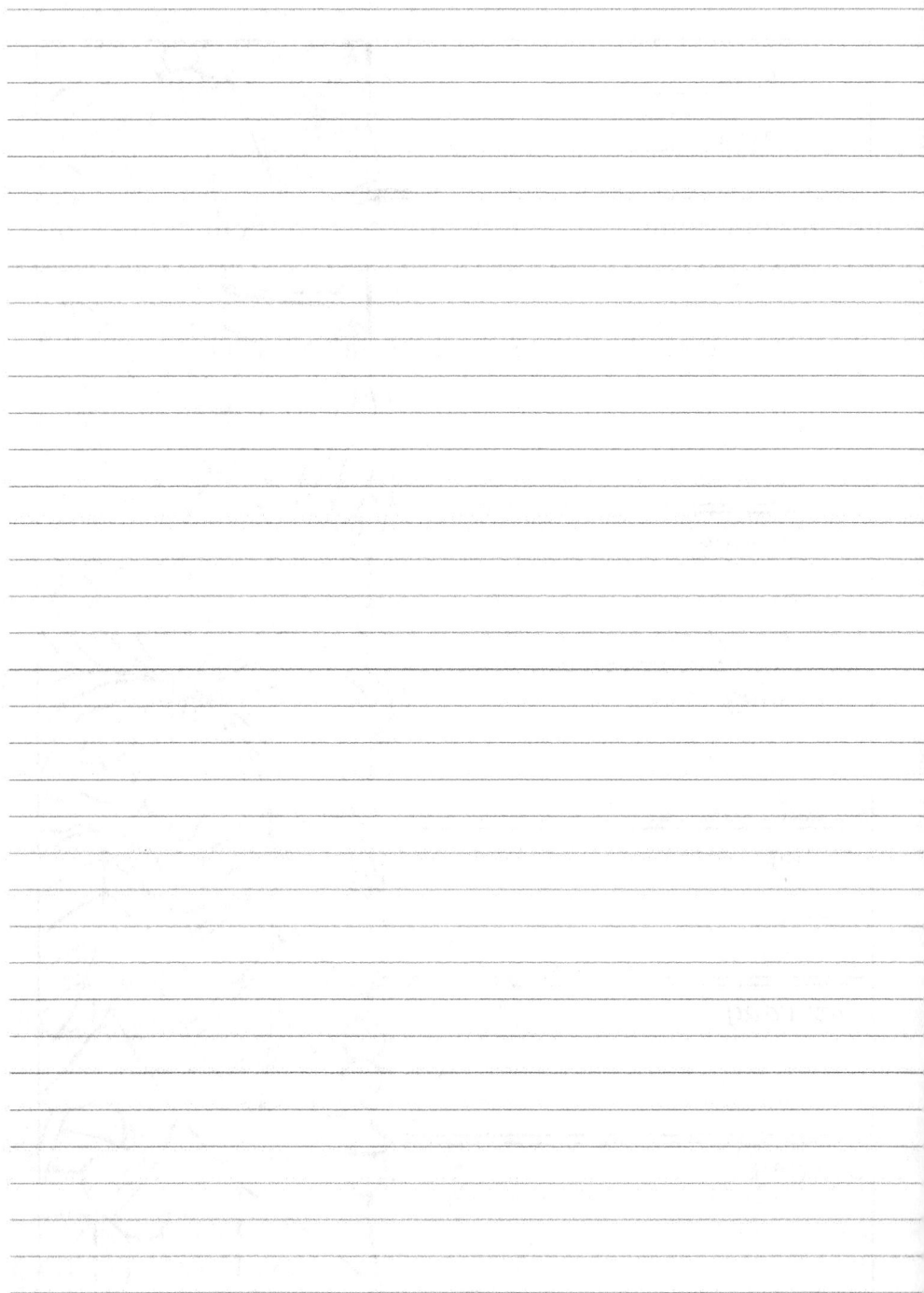

From _____ to _____

Month _____ Year _____

Monday

Tuesday

Wednesday

Thursday

Friday

Saturday

Sunday

From _____ to _____

Month _____ Year _____

Monday

Tuesday

Wednesday

Thursday

Friday

Saturday

Sunday

From _____ to _____

Month _____ Year _____

Monday

Tuesday

Wednesday

Thursday

Friday

Saturday

Sunday

From _____ to _____

Month _____ Year _____

Monday

Tuesday

Wednesday

Thursday

Friday

Saturday

Sunday

From _____ to _____

Month _____ Year _____

Monday

Tuesday

Wednesday

Thursday

Friday

Saturday

Sunday

From _____ to _____

Month _____ Year _____

Monday

Tuesday

Wednesday

Thursday

Friday

Saturday

Sunday

From _____ to _____

Month _____ Year _____

Monday

Tuesday

Wednesday

Thursday

Friday

Saturday

Sunday

From _____ to _____

Month _____ Year _____

Monday

Tuesday

Wednesday

Thursday

Friday

Saturday

Sunday

From _____ to _____

Month _____ Year _____

Monday

Tuesday

Wednesday

Thursday

Friday

Saturday

Sunday

From _____ to _____

Month _____ Year _____

Monday

Tuesday

Wednesday

Thursday

Friday

Saturday

Sunday

From _____ to _____

Month _____ Year _____

Monday

Tuesday

Wednesday

Thursday

Friday

Saturday

Sunday

From _____ to _____

Month _____ Year _____

Monday

Tuesday

Wednesday

Thursday

Friday

Saturday

Sunday

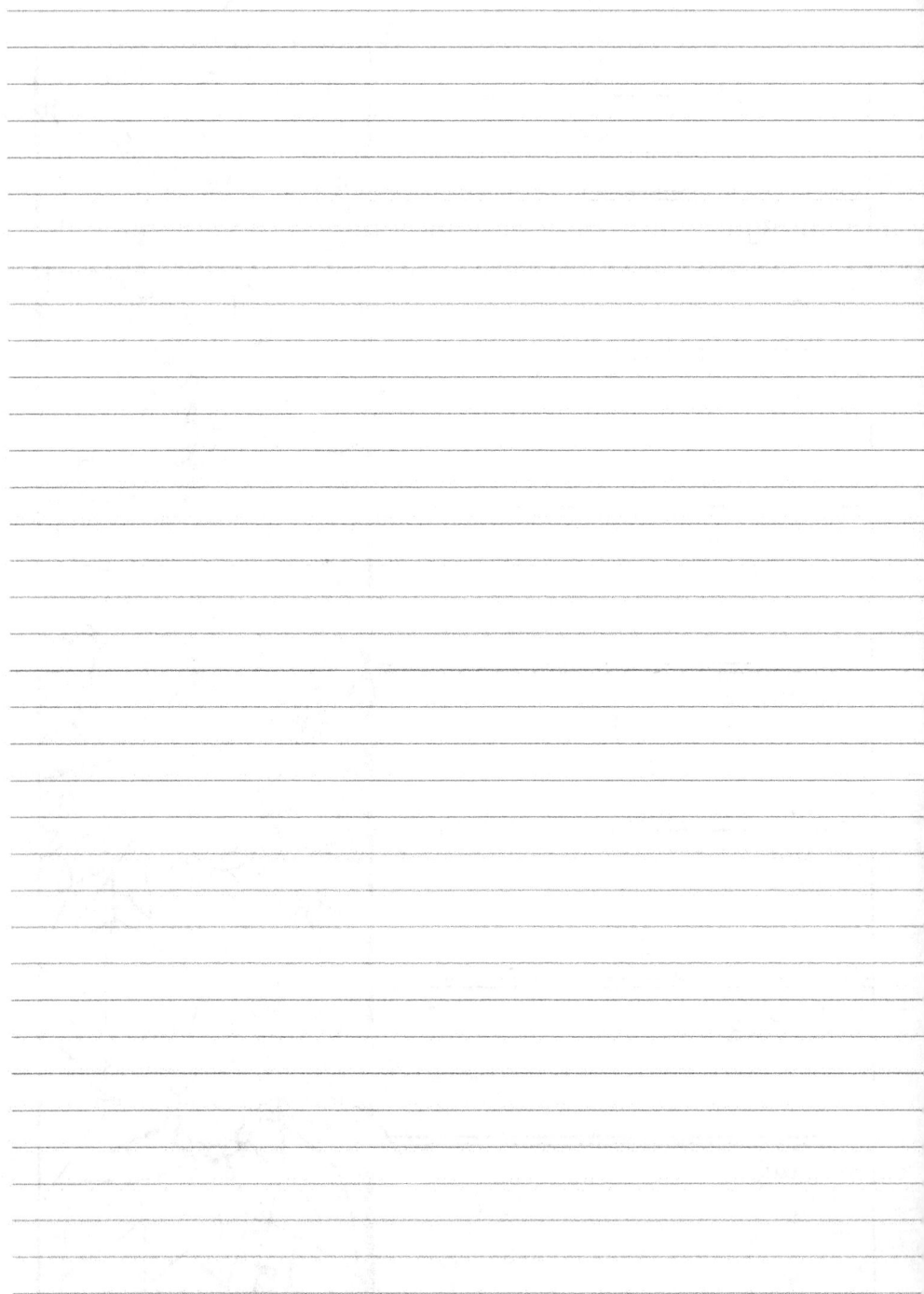

From _____ to _____

Month _____ Year _____

Monday

Tuesday

Wednesday

Thursday

Friday

Saturday

Sunday

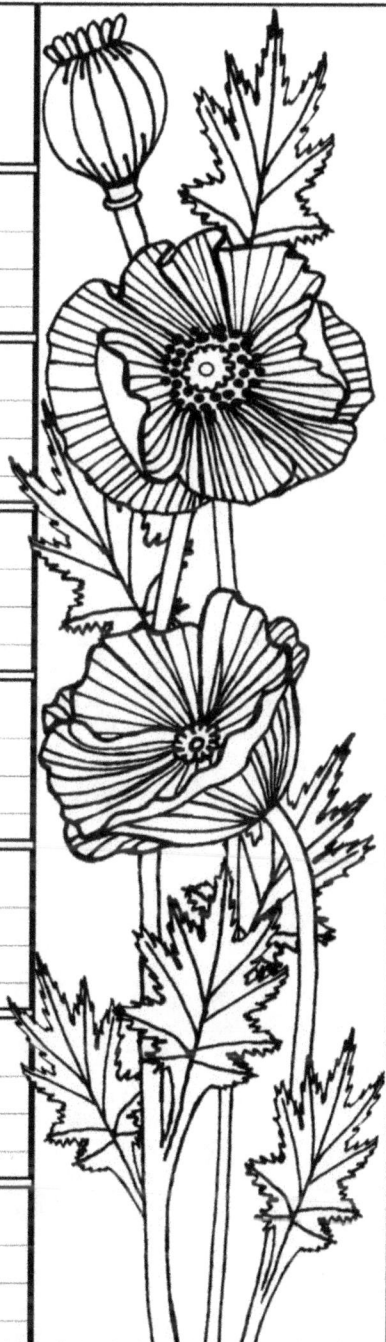

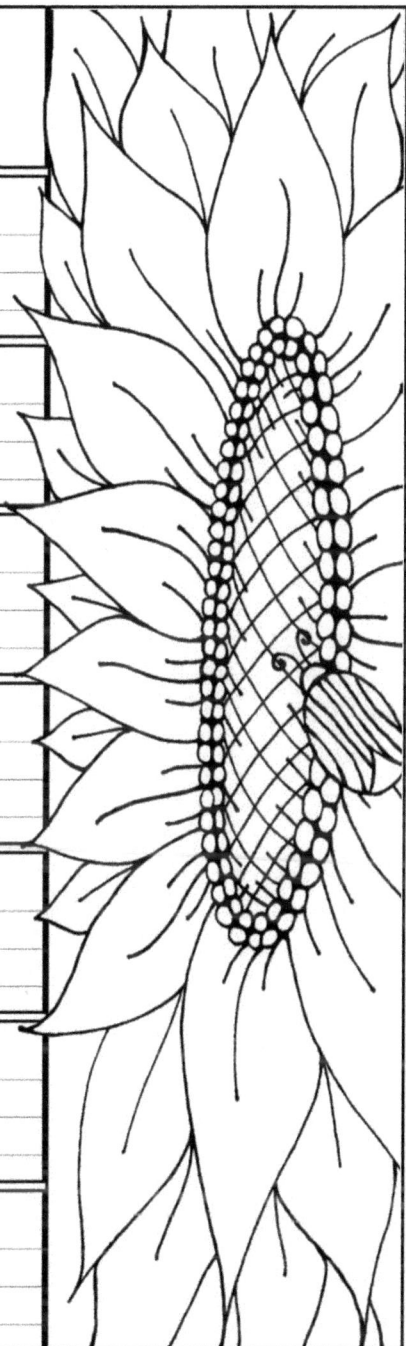

From _____ to _____

Month _____ Year _____

Monday

Tuesday

Wednesday

Thursday

Friday

Saturday

Sunday

From _____ to _____

Month _____ Year _____

Monday

Tuesday

Wednesday

Thursday

Friday

Saturday

Sunday

From _____ to _____

Month _____ Year _____

Monday

Tuesday

Wednesday

Thursday

Friday

Saturday

Sunday

From _____ to _____

Month _____ Year _____

Monday

Tuesday

Wednesday

Thursday

Friday

Saturday

Sunday

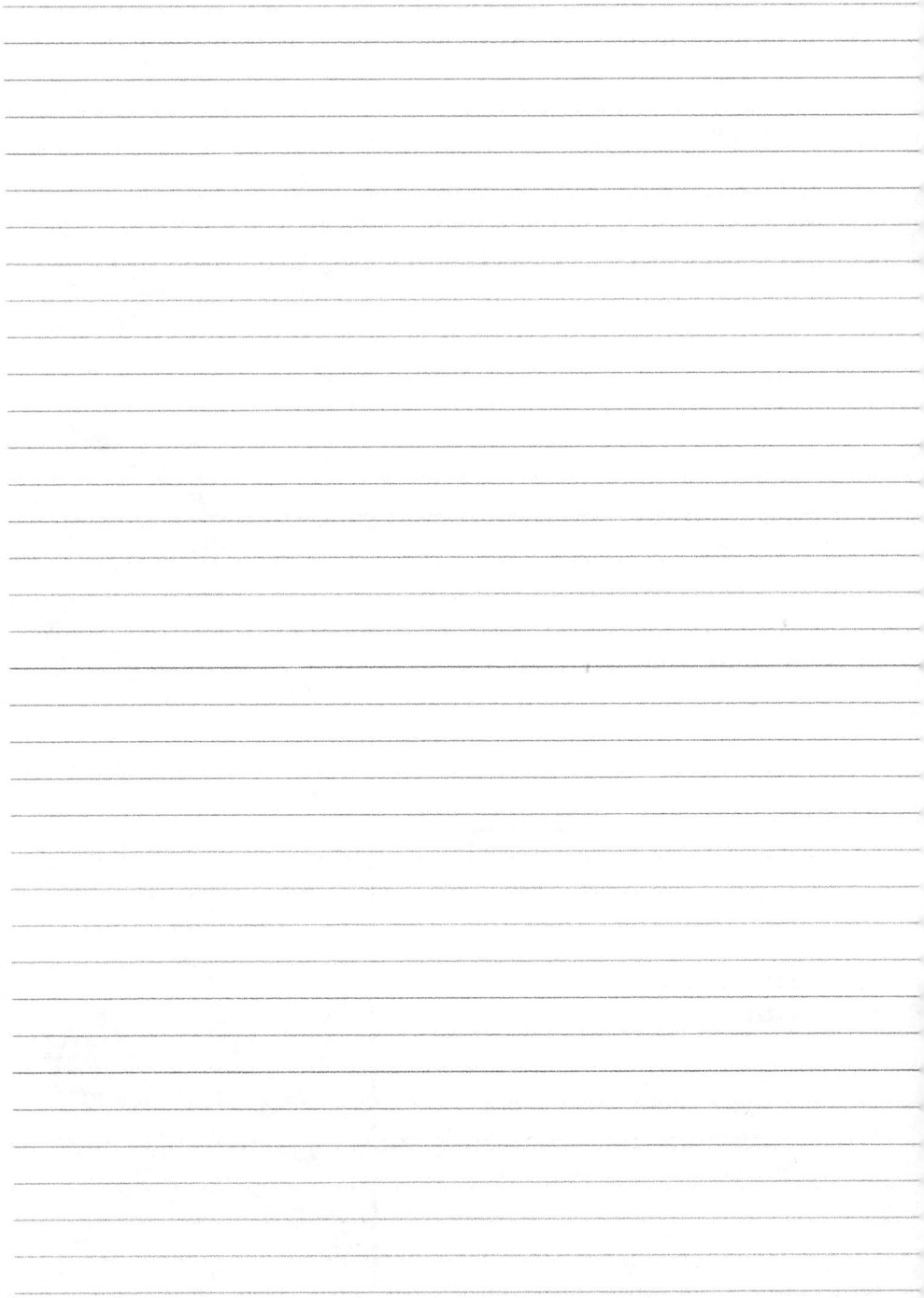

From _____ to _____

Month _____ Year _____

Monday

Tuesday

Wednesday

Thursday

Friday

Saturday

Sunday

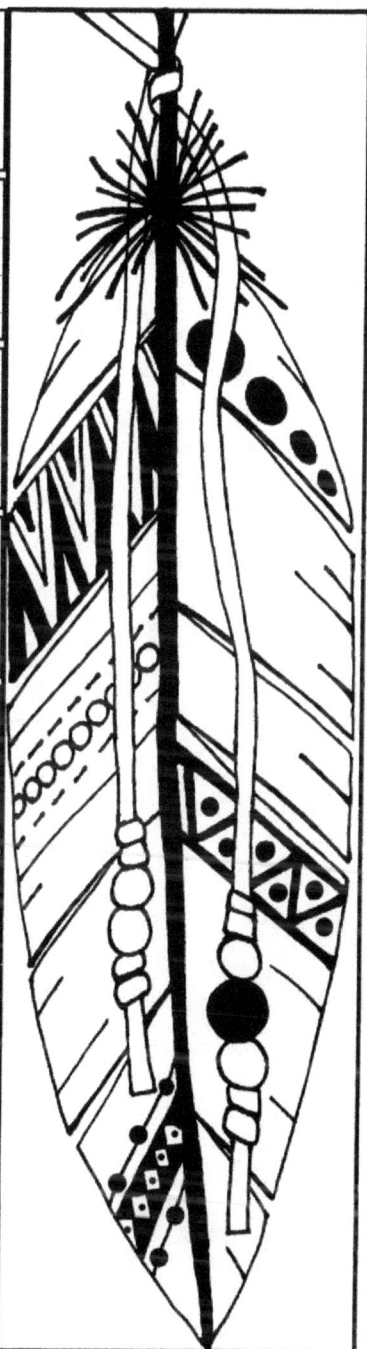

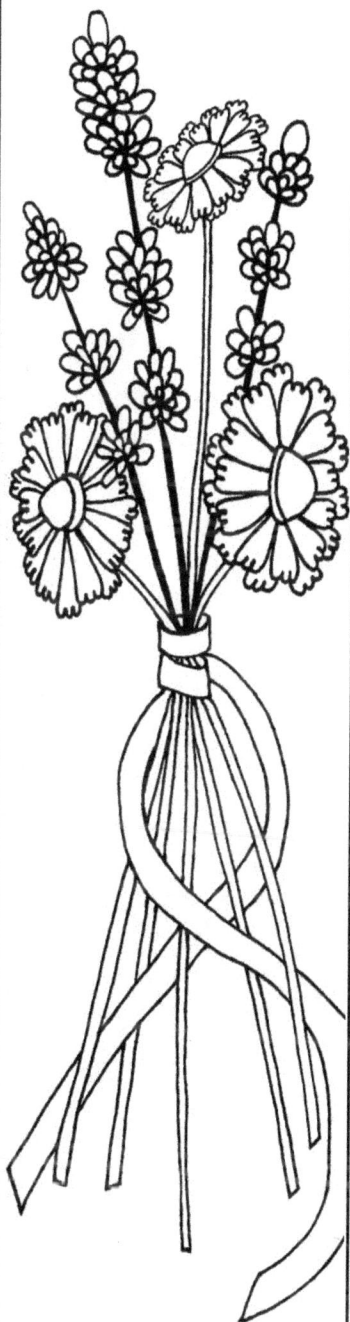

From _____ to _____

Month _____ Year _____

Monday

Tuesday

Wednesday

Thursday

Friday

Saturday

Sunday

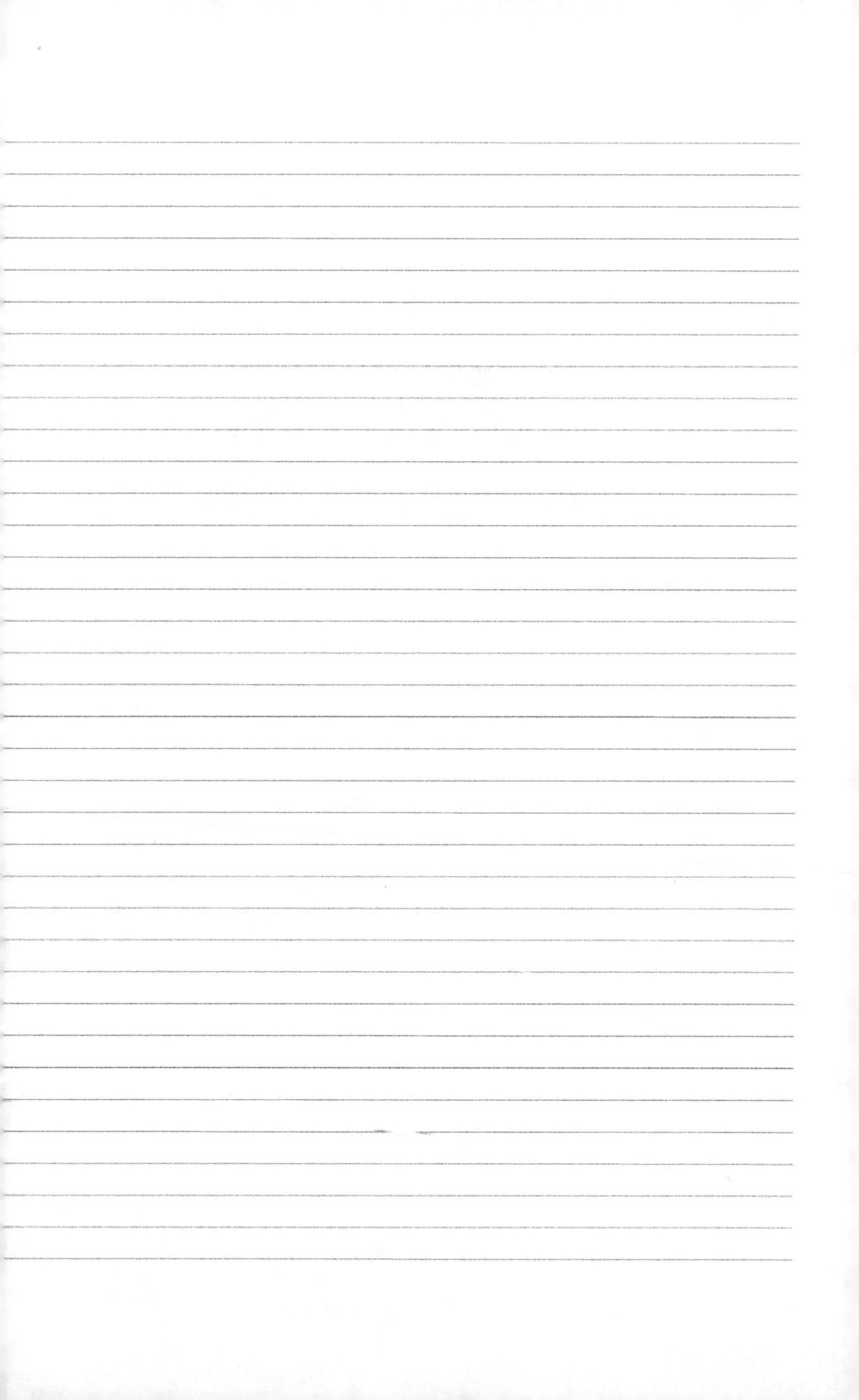

◈◆◈

Enjoying this Coloring Planner?
Please leave me a review.
I would love to hear your feedback.
Thank you for purchasing my product.
You support is greatly appreciated.

◈◈◆◈◈

www.ingramcontent.com/pod-product-compliance
Lightning Source LLC
Chambersburg PA
CBHW060818050426
42449CB00008B/1719